MW00379581

Thoughts

from the

Journey

Elizabeth L. Hudgins

TO MARY MACPHERSON
A FAITHFUL FRIEND
A SOLID EDITOR
A WITNESS OF GRACE

Introduction

There's been a riot in my mind.
One dead, four wounded, and a baby crying, abandoned.
The roads twist off in varied directions,
Wandering distractedly through the old city.
Stores and houses crowd the narrow street,
Squat remembrances of ancient times.
In the distance a cathedral spire soars into the sky,
Filled with holy wonder as light pierces
The stained glass patterns,
Tracing stories on the floor within.
I try daily to visit it,
To rise above the hovels
And trash-strewn doorways,
To stand among the arches
And contemplate the patterned glass.
Sometimes I find a road that leads from the confusion
Of twists and turns to the cathedral close.
Most times, though, I end wandering the maze
Of narrow streets until the twilight settles in.
Still, though I often find
Bleeding ideas and riot-torn arguments,
I know that somewhere in that city that is I,
A concept slowly grows,
Beginning to move into the heavens.

The Incarnation

King Jesus,
    Was it as heavy as I think
        For You to wrap Yourself in human
            form,
    You who sang the stars into existence
        And formed man from the clay?
    Did You feel imprisoned
        When You walked on dusty roads
And knew human weariness,
        Thinking human thoughts
        And knowing human fears?
    Locked in human life forever,
        Did You see Your carpenter's hands
            Blistered from working wood
        And know that greater wounds
            Were figured there?
Lord Jesus,
    Was bearing the cross
        A greater burden
            Than wearing human flesh?

The Grammar of Faith

for Liz

Conjugating faith descriptively
        (Christ has died,
        Christ is risen,
        Christ will come again)
    Leaves little room
    For little faith in need of
        Strong aorist[1] verbs.
Oh yes, for proper form,
    Carefully parse each verse,
        Hanging infinitives on curves and
        Perching adjectives on slides,
    But set the subjects, predicates, and objects
        On bold, straight lines
For I need grammar both
        Generative
        And transformational[2]

1. Aorist is a verb form in Ancient and Koina Greek which states an action with no reference to an ending or duration.

2. Generative and Transformational are types of linguistic "grammars" where the sentence structure is discussed in terms of building blocks of meaning units.

Hope of Glory

You speak of plucking eyes
And chopping hands that offend
And I know that You have not gone far enough,
For I have ears and tongue and feet
And even heart that need to go.
What then? When no sinew remains,
No bone, no skin? When all is gone,
And I have nothing left?
May I come stand with You,
And looking back on these dry, scattered bones,
Dare hope for them to live again?
I would prefer, instead, to find more certain hope:
A new life altogether
And holiness that's His.

Spirit Wings

There's danger in flying too near the Son.
    Waxed wings melt
    And flight comes feather-crashing down.
But if, perchance,
    The wings were not of wax,
    Son-flying life might
    Burn in altar-offered joy.

Answers

A sterile time...
   Dry and brown.
Even rising from kneeling prayer
Brought empty pain.
So much promise
Yet so loud the silence.
He shuffled down the aisle
Then, pushing the carved door open,
Limped into the heavy day.

Behind him
Sunlight pierced a pane defect
And shattered,
Bleeding rainbow shards of glory
On the wooden door.

Isaiah Knew

Isaiah knew the smell of incense,
Felt the burning coal cleanse lips.
He heard the
"HOLY, HOLY, HOLY"
Chanted from every corner,
Echoing in his every cell.

One day, though,
The angels left their post
To stand in a sheep field
In the dark of night
And cry "Glory to God in the highest."
Knowing the songs to be the same,
He yearned to understand the HOLY
Becoming Child.

Nativity Set

Bethlehem's offering—
   A wooden nativity set.
   The little cruciform baby Jesus,
    Arms outstretched,
    Perchance to welcome shepherds.
Around the crib kneel
   Wooden shepherds,
   Stately wooden kings,
   And an olive-wood Mary,
"Made in Bethlehem"
Stamped carefully on each piece.

Time slows,
   Carved patiently,
Made in Jerusalem
   Of wood
     And nails.

The Gift

The Kingdom of God rushed wind down,
Uprooting preconceived
In Baby King's conception.
Isaiah's ancient songs
Echoed down the hills,
As Seraphim cried out,
And Cherubim proclaimed.
Below, in gathering wind,
I wrapped my cloak
Against the night,
Feeling the altar fire star
Kiss earth,
And burdens made forever light
By God
In Christmas giving.

Thank God

She offered the flour of her youth,
And God took it
   To make a house of Bread.
Thank God for Bethlehem.[1]
And God the King,
   When the time had come,
   Walked dusty roads
   Toward Jerusalem to take the cross
   And make our peace.
Thank God for Jerusalem.[2]
Later that week, Jesus knelt in a garden,
 Sweating drops of Blood,
   Pressed in spirit,
   As He set His face to die.
Thank God for Gethsemane.[3]

1. Bethlehem means "House of Bread".

2. Jerusalem means "Hearth of Peace".

3. Gethsemane means "Olive Press".

Dancing with Angels

I've danced with angels,
   Woven an intricate step
   Until the first rays of dawn.
I've wrestled them too,
   Held firm in their burning touch,
And heard their whispered words
   In a room filled with wings.
I've seen them spinning and bowing
   Like dust in a crisp spring sun
   Or leaves playing in the wind.
I've known the hosts of angel warriors
   With their fiery chariots,
And watched one angel
   Waiting patiently, sitting on a stone,
   To say, "He is not here".

Jigsaw Puzzles

When the last day arrives,
When the resurrection occurs,
The puzzles will be astounding!
All those small pieces of saints—
Those who became fish food
Or ashes dusting the seas or hills,
And best of all, the canonized:
A finger here, a skull there...
Tourist trade
And pilgrim hope.
Bits and pieces everywhere!
The pattern won't be difficult,
After all, He's done it before:
"The ankle bone's connected to the...."
But with the sound of a trumpet,
All those parts reunite,
Transfigured
In the twinkling of an eye,
Everything in its assigned place,
The puzzles complete.

On Seeing the Stars at Night

Her face is dark skinned like the Black Madonna,
And yet I know she's filled with light like grace.
She shimmers with the royalty of fleur-de-lis stars
Even as she grows great with the fruit of expanding suns,
And though her face is dark as Kedar's tents,
I know that she is lovely as the curtains of Solomon.
So I yearn, this dark night soul,
To embrace her light invisible
And ride the solar wind in joy
Until I know in heart and mind and soul
That all shall be well.

The Crucifer

For Merle

The crucifer, tonsured by time,
Lifts high the cross
And leads to hallowed spaces,
Following blood-stained steps
Made fresh each day in anamnesis,
And a broken hand
Gives broken bread
That holds the heart of God.

Going Home

Once wrapped in wealth and hope,
Undeserving yet proud,
His youth and weakness
Proved the familiar story.
Soon he sat ragged in a pig sty.
Friends deserted him,
Not even staying to point out his errors
As Job's had.
The only similarity being the dung heaps.
Tired of poverty
And his parched-voice dreams,
He headed home,
The smell of pigs still clinging.
With each step he rehearsed:
I was wrong.
I am sorry.
Make me a servant.
Drawing near,
He could hear the cry of the turtledove:
The winter is past, the rains over,
A fatted calf awaited slaughter.

Ezekiel 36

"I have profaned His Name among the heathen."

Do you know,
Image bearer marred by birthmark,
That your steps scar,
Spreading image-like in your wake,
Your features, distorted
As in a broken mirror?

So sigh grew earth voiced,
Waiting for sons to walk
As when the Light
Entered clay,
Reflecting image purely.

A secret thing,
Hawthorne known,
Healing birthmark brings death,
But death, unblemishing, brings life.

The Second Coming

Few noticed the first coming...
    A handful of shepherds,
    Several wise men (a little late),
    And a host of angels,
A few people,
And all of heaven.

At the second coming,
    The proud will be scattered,
    All knees will bow,
    The Mount of Olives will quake
    So the earth splits east to west,
    And the gate so long blocked
    By feet of brick and stone
Will open
For the King to come into His city.

Between times?
His Church will wait with hope
For a trumpet sound
To rend the air.

Elementary I

Wind, fire, and water
  All are Spirit tied,
  But never earth alone.
    Earth is man's domain.
But wind blows where it will,
Fire tongues dance holiness,
And water gushes from the Rock.
Spirit moves freely,
  Creating, permeating,
  Indwelling
  So earth vessels come alive.

Elementary II

Earth is man's domain
And takes a clay-locked God
   To touch its heart.
Wind, fire, and water are Spirit life.
   Wind shakes loose
   The prison chains of men,
   Fire tongues speak
   Into earth wrought
   Water courses out from wounded Rock.
Earthborn,
By God-man sacrifice,
Becomes heaven named.

Bread and Wine

Bread and wine
Require not just death
To harvest.
Each must suffer.
Grain crushed.
Oil pressed.
Grapes stomped.
Just so the Bread of Life
Must go to Gethsemane:
Pressed and sweating blood
Under the weight of saying yes.

Questions

Scholars were full of questions—
   Why the meek would inherit,
   Why He ate with sinners,
   How He fed 5,000.
Some had witnessed,
   Had seen Him lift five small loaves,
    Give thanks,
    And break them,
   And none left hungry.
Yes, the Pharisees had questions,
But Jesus never answered them.
One day they finally nailed Him down,
Lifted Him, broke Him.
Rumor has it He still breaks bread.
The Pharisees still have questions,
But the hungry continue to come
   And are filled.

Transfiguration

Wrapped in Father's love,
Arms stretched to worship God,
Flesh pores could not restrain
God glory/man joy,
Broken bonds
Transfused even rough weave cloak
With light/Shekinah.

Presenting Church

Palestrina and Gounod,
Thomas Tallis...
Our choir are paid professionals.
Our lectors, trained
In diction and pacing,
Read the lessons with
Modulated tones,
Drama trained.
Even the ushers
Move in perfect unison.
The sermon, fifteen minutes,
Never more,
Speaks of good things...
Prosperity and happiness.
A gash-gold vermillion
Interrupting—
A rumbled cry:
"Lazarus, Come forth!"

The Cloisters

Fort Tryon Park, NY

The museum built above the Hudson
Of old world chapel parts
And monastic community sections
Ripped, labelled, and packed
Now, carefully reconstructed
And displayed
On this foreign soil.
Stones, which should have cried out
Glory and Honor,
Sit quietly,
Purpose lost or confused.
Sometimes a chant,
Piped through the latest sound system,
Hovers almost silent.

Back on the subway,
I hurtle under Brooklyn
While above me
Men with sidelocks,
Long black coats,
And beards,
Dance the Sabbath with great joy.

Ascension Thursday

The sun thundered out at dawn
    With the fierce, bright precision
    Of an Old Testament prophet
      Shouting out God's Word
      Into the still grey air.
No cloud proclaimed His coming,
    Elijah-like,
    In gold-rose hues.
Today He did not come in clouds;
    He came in piercing, burning light
    And wheat-warm Host.
The Son thundered out in glory,
    And tongues of fire proclaimed His dawn.

All Hallows

Today grey light drizzles,
Muting colors
Which just last week
Shouted brilliance
From flaming trees.
Now the latter rain's behind
And autumn's fog
Softens sounds
As well as light.
All Saints Day,
And from the damp chill mist,
All Hallows still
Chant quiet prayers
With incense praise
That, in their midst,
Hallowed be Thy Name.

Holy Week
Spain

Sun warmed streets
Where Maimonides and the Greek walked.
    Thought and textures—
The business of the men.
One pondered reason
The other pictured lunatics,
Where Moors built a synagogue for Jews
And flagellants still ply their shard-toothed thongs.

One bleak Good Friday
I watched a tourist climb awkwardly
Across a kneeling penitent,
Only concerned to see a relic ring finger.
Pilgrimages, religious or tourist.

Metaphysics says little in the day
Where hallowed shadows
Speak silently in stones
Rising in Gothic glory.

Bones and Breath

The Tanakh[1]
Originally written in consonants only,
Fodder for reflection,
But difficult to read.
Consonants stop sound,
Leaving dry bones waiting vowels
For breath.
Ezekiel 37 knows.
Calling
    The wind,
    The breath,
    The Spirit
To blow across this dry-bone page,
Lifting consonants,
    Bringing words to life,
    Allowing them to sing
    Urging them to soar.

1. The Jewish Bible/the Old Testament

Reading Scripture

On the Sabbath,
Jews read a Parsha, a portion,
Of the Torah.
A feast to be chewed
And all week word grown
With pondering possibilities,
Nosing into corners
And playing with ideas,
Yet knowing text truth.

On Sunday,
Christians, too, read a passage
Of the Bible,
Seeking theological
Through text truth doors.
A passage meant to be traversed.

I'm trying to read both portion and passage.

Coming to Abraham,
The battle won and Lot rescued,
The plot battle told
Moves toward home
In the darkness of night.
The warriors must have been war weary.

Suddenly a priest/king appears,
Melchizedek named.
Abraham gifts a tithe to him,
And he gives bread and wine.

Suddenly the text interrupts,
Crying out:
"A tithe? After the battle victory?
Did he bring a caravan to hold it all?"

And another voice says,
"He was a picture, a type, of Christ!
He brought bread and wine,
communion,
And he received a tithe offering!"

And I smiled, enjoying God's presence
As I read.

Comments on Overtones

For Olida

Sing your note gently,
Warm and round in hope.
Hold it carefully and wait.
For a note, like life, begets another
And that another still,
Note upon note and tone within tone,
If we had ears to hear
We would know the ripples grow,
Filling our space with mystery
Far greater than even the glory we see.
For even the rocks cry out in sympathetic joy,
And trees clap hands in awe
With the harmony of these spheres,
Rising like incense into the vaults and groins
Of great cathedrals and, yes, beyond.

Pentecost

Separate
Words prayed behind door-locked night
Or wept in tear-streaked hope
Until
Flame fused,
Bone to bone and sinew set
In wind-danced flame,
Together
One word
In many tongues proclaimed.

Seasons

In fall
Every tree becomes a burning bush.
Quickly, as though the limbs can't bear the heat,
The fiery leaf tongues drop.

Trees grow still,
With only a whispered rattle in the wind.
They wait patiently
The quiet white blanket.

Autumn left so rapidly,
But winter stays,
A stark white.

Suddenly,
The small green upheaval—
Dry, hard ground ruptured
By tiny blade's piercing.
Pollen green's new leaves erupt,

Replaced too soon
By summer's unrelenting fire.

Transition times have O so short a call,
As though the color bursts take all.

Road to Emmaus

Early in the day
Reading meant breaking a code—
Turning sight to sound,
Stammering syllables from stylus scratches—
A miracle of meaning.
Then, becoming more adept,
Reaching through the page
To touch and hear,
See and sometimes even smell
A world incarnate by word.
Later, as teachers know,
Reading grew larger still
Layered with allusions
And ripe with allegory,
Text nosed tome,
Prodding meaning and questioning hopes,
Until cacophony sorted
In rubric edges of interwoven script
Finally, rabbis and priests taught glosses—
Scholarly methods where shadow types print truth
For those who parse it out,
Signposts with each word holding greater mystery.
At dusk, weary from the journey
Yet heady with the work,
My heart burned within me,
And in the breaking of this bread,
I am home.

Word Hoard

Words shuffle along
Like brittle old folks out for a walk,
Stumbling in motley garb,
Struggling to bear the weight of meaning
Until joints creak tearfully
And the wraggle-tag parade limps into sight.
Acrobats too old to dance
Crash sadly into clowns.
Yet in the midst of the awkward show
The Word becomes flesh
And dwells among us.

Holy Words

For druids all words set down on rock,
Cut deep or not,
Were holy words—
The writing made it so.
My words suffer in hope for holy.
My pen tacks down the writhing line,
Searching to find a word
For thoughts still shifting
And a place for phrases turned out homeless.
I hope for holy words
Illuminated gloriously,
With gold and balanced design.
Instead I find a tortured line
Twisting meaning
Out of dust,
Written poorly with an old pen.

Language

Incubated words
Begin crawling from the dark,
Small creatures
Blinking at the light of day,
Meaning awakening in the eye.
In youth—nouns:
    Dog   Cat
Then, branching out, verbs:
    Run   Eat
But how to jump to abstract thoughts?
To past and future tenses?
Hypotheticals?
When do they become aware of beauty in sound?
How did words discover poetry
And struggle into art,
Nestling quietly into poems?

Teaching Poetry

When I look at my class,
Twenty-one boys and five girls,
I wonder how so many poets have been men.
Visions of grey-haired laureates
With elbows suede patched
Fade,
Replaced by baseball-cap laurels
And jeans where knees peek through ragged fringe.
My students want no poetry.
Books are scarce.
Yet words tumble incessantly
As tongues rush on like ribbons flashing in the wind,
Flogged by trite whips and thoughts.
Their language like their bodies, sprawls,
Held together with jargon bones and curse-word sinews.
Still, tomorrow's poet may be hiding here,
Waiting to fall into a world of words set free
Like banners puffed by rushing winds.

Work in Progress

I watch the black ink-crosshatched slough patiently.
A thesaurus list of words hangs,
Snake like,
From an unseen limb above the fen,
And I wander the edge,
Gathering fuel for future use.
Waiting, as men and women watch the shore
For the tortoises to hatch,
Daring to think this hoped-for child will birth,
Believing it will develop legs and drag itself to shore,
Yet hoping always for wings instead so it can soar.

Writer's Block

Careful excavation of old journals
Has yielded no grand treasure,
Not even a small pottery shard
With which to play.
I've even dropped clever images,
Hoping some idea would follow them home
Out of curiosity and stay for tea if not for poem.
I've sifted past crime scenes
Of discarded lines,
Looking for a thread to follow,
And I've waded through files of great lines
I haven't found a home for yet
(They're still orphans waiting adoption),
And tried flipping through computer listings,
Looking for a topic to expand, anything.
So far the page remains pristine.

Solitude

One stands apart—
Gauntly dark and angular.
Few choose his company—
He lacks the skill of social banter.
Few even look him in the eyes—
They're brown—a study in silences.
Life's reserved.
The smallest nod inviting,
And I self-consciously accept.
His arms are strong and sure,
Surprisingly certain as we move
To music made of bone and tendon rather than hearing,
Long bowing strokes meeting woodwind breath
In sinewy tango.
There are no tentative moves
In Solitude's strong lead,
The glides and dips familiar
As my heartbeat—
Revealing a dance I must have known
But only now have named.
I relax in his strength,
Confident of these steps
In a dance not made for crowds.

Dance Macabre

After the plague years,
Printers let Death dance
In the margins of books,
Relegating him to the edge of our lives—
A safe place, considering.
Yet diminishing death proved harder
Than sacrificing margins.
When least expected, he invades
Our ordered texts,
Disrupting our careful plots
With his cruel endings.

Forty Days

Morning light swells
To the sharp edge of noon,
An Old Testament prophet's fiery eye
Battering the young shoots
Until they shrivel,
Brittle before their time.
Thirsty, not living by bread alone,
Jesus trod these sun-parched hills,
Tempted even by wave of oasis lies.
Slowly the blistering light withdraws,
Leaving remorseless cold,
The vicious stab
Of a Bedouin night,
And the silence of stars.

Light

Like a child after rain
Looking for puddles in which to play,
Light seeks small drops of water
Then leaps into them, splashing rainbows
Across the sky...
Sometimes even two,
The second being a mirror image of the first.
She bends a pole in water,
Or so it looks.
It's magic!
In northern climes she,
Apparently bored with winter chill,
Duplicates the sun,
Presenting three side by side.
The middle one is real:
It's not a shell game.
From casting colors
To painting everything,
She works that magic.
Yet she never takes a bow,
Choosing instead to hide in plain sight.

Recalling

When the honeysuckle captured the fences,
I, lost in the cloying sweetness, suddenly was back
In the warm, long, barefoot days
Sitting on a makeshift raft with Flo.
Our lake, little more than half an acre,
Snuggled securely amidst sentinel trees.
Bamboo poled us on our lazy journey.
We were Huck and Tom,
And the light of our days was hot and crusty.
Later, with the raft docked and summer nearly spent,
The crabapples fell in squishy brown roundness.
We, and the bees, were drawn by the cider sweetness.
Playing dodge ball with these rotting missiles,
Made serious by the threat of sting and start of school,
We ran, laughing and screaming, into fall.

Surf Fishing

My father taught me to love surf fishing
And the warmth of life at the shore,
But my joy was casting the line,
Seeing it leap from the old Chesapeake reel,
Watching its sharp line dance light
In an arc reaching beyond the waves.
The movement, the sheer glory!
I know the pull of the line pregnant with dinner,
The dance of the catch.
Others can play it carefully to shore,
Let me cast the line.

My People

Bohemian polkas and homebrewed beer
Are mine by birthright from my mother's people—
Solid Mid-Western Republican farmers with Union ties.
My father's watermen, all Democrats
Convinced the South will rise again,
Bequeathed sweet tea and Sunday parlors
With quiet and staid antimacassars.
They met as foreigners barely able to understand
Each other's language,
Similarities limited to small, hard wintergreens
In pressed glass dishes,
Children, and poverty.

Drafted Service

Children of the Depression,
My parents believed in second callings.
What served today, straightforward and assured,
Appeared, without apology, tomorrow in a new work.
Small cheese jars of this afternoon
Overnight became morning juice containers.
Those were magic times.
Empty jars stood in military precision on shelves
Just waiting to guard nails to be hammered
Someday into greatness,
Or pens for writing novels,
Or even rubber bands for shooting
Or holding things together.
Even my sister's diapers,
When no longer serving their first post,
Offered dishtowel service, soft and thirsty.
When, in the enthusiastic days of middle school,
I dreamed of lepidopterist honors,
A diaper volunteered, along with an old hanger
And a broom handle no longer in active duty,
To serve as my butterfly net.
My parents were ardent pioneer recyclers.
Any environmentalist would have applauded.

Piecemaker

In memory of Amy Howlett Borland

Telling her frugal life, piece by ragged piece,
Sewing log cabins and flying geese
In textile beauty, the old quilt maker
Passed her retirement from raising turkeys
In the harsh summers and cruel winters
Of Nebraska's Sandhills
And teaching hardy children
In one room schools with little heat.
She was seasoned by hardships
And gentled by her love of nature.
Her fingers, gnarled and bony,
Made small even stitches,
And, when stiffened by the labor,
Turned the pages of the Wall Street Journal
To check on her portfolio.

August 6, 1945

In memory of Major Theodore "Dutch" Van Kirk
Navigator of the Enola Gay

Called from their fields,
Different in ancestry as in trades,
The eleven came—
Forged together by chance and destiny,
Steeled to work as one.
Their plane rises against the dark,
The growl of the engines familiar and strong,
A young Dutch plows the night
Until their sowing's done.
Behind, a mushroom pushes
From the earth—
A crop to end a war.

Saturday Nights in Georgetown in the '60s

We packed the smoke-filled clubs,
College students drawn by live jazz and beer.
We were a generation enamored of ourselves.
Soon the boys became men
In a jungle of politics and war,
And our music grew angry,
Forcing us into the streets
Of a world we did not know,
Where honor rode on buses,
Courage sat at lunch counters,
And music grew in protest and hope.

Nantucket Watercolor

The rust-red bicycle etched its way,
Decisive and sure purposed.
The rider splashed towards town
For pen and ink
To carve this night
A craggy poem
Gouged with sharp-edge words
And streaks of fire.

Light II

Morning light dances,
Dappling tree leaves,
Playing gently until noon.
Then it blazes,
Burning the day
With its powerful eye.
Later the light withdraws.
We turn lamps on—
Light's weak remembrances,
Hand-colored and faded,
But conveniently tame
And comfortably certain.

Desert Dust

Carrying small shards of our Bedouin world,
The showers of April
Pall entire European cities
With our finest Arabian dust
Even as the Gobi
Quietly takes Beijing in its loess,
Naming the Yellow River in its wake.
From the rime of winter
To this near silent invasion,
We live our lives,
And no matter how carefully we dust,
We find our springs in deserts.

Old Age

Age sneaks up quietly,
A feral creature,
Stalking purposefully,
Unnoticed.

My body knows,
Recognizing the creeping beast,
Telling its presence
In groans and joint-twisted pain.

My mind, concerned with other thoughts,
Has no awareness,
No clue of the beast.
When will I grow up?
I don't feel any older:
I'm still the same as I was at 16...
Same thoughts, same me.

Friends I haven't seen for several years
Seem so old when I see them suddenly now—
Aged reticulated faces sagging and fragile.
It happened when I wasn't looking,
Totally relaxed and happy in my quiet world.
Aging and death are foreign to us
And totally unexpected.

Cancer

For George

"Cancer," the doctor said,
And the word hung in the air,
A vapor of pestilence and fear.
I found no poesy
Eased my breath,
Which caught and choked.
He lanced the bubo
To send to the pathologist,
Wrapping the tissue gently
As though it were the fragile part.
We watched you, carefully checking your humors,
Waiting for any telltale sign of illness.
We clothed our apprehension
In smiles of confidence and comfort,
But fear, a systemic poison, grew
And we rushed to shut the door on our possible loss,
Burying our thoughts in talk of politics and work.

Requiem

As you lay there, skin slack upon the bones
And jaundiced by age and illness,
Your ragged, shallow breath became a mantra in my heart.
You waited, patiently,
As though time didn't exist,
While I sat anxiously,
Feeling it rush, a monsoon-swollen stream
Too deep to wade across.
At odd times tears came,
Interludes in a world set deep
In drunken joys and silent stillnesses of faith.
Now, in the midst of this world
Grown colder by your absence,
The shock of missing you
Still surprises with its sudden power.

Moving On

They moved out slowly, my parents,
Road map veins marking detours and disasters.
Memories were packed and shipped,
All but a few which became the focus.
Their skin grew fragile and cooler to my touch
So that a coroner might begin to calculate
My loss.
I shut the door on the inevitable
Yet could not, from superstitious fear,
Throw the deadbolt.
They disassociated, and I,
Not knowing that ritual,
Grew angry and embarrassed for them.
One day, as if relieved,
They sighed peacefully and left.

Fading Memory

Like an old guitarist,
Faded jeans and gray-dusted hair,
Strumming the past....
Fingers calloused by the strings.
Toes tap rhythms forgotten by the mind
Yet known in every nerve
As sure as his heartbeat—
Everything lost but that song.

Memories

The cozy cave under the belly of the baby grand
Invited us in those between times
When all was done
But the waiting for Dad for dinner,
Then the "Black Hawk Waltz"
Would leap from Mom's fingers,
Enveloping our warmth
With a god's rumbling voice
Carving space between times
With its magic three-four thunder.

Gene's Place

I love those bushel baskets,
Wire-bent handles bleeding age down darkened slats.
The rims sun-splashed, promise harvests
Like hands expectant,
And in the breeze a hint,
Even this early spring
When snowdrops and jonquils prod the earth,
Rattling our shortening dark with hope
Of Winesap and cider.

Safari

I expected eyes
Rousseau-like
Piercing the thick dark of snaking vines.
Instead I found creatures hidden in plain sight—
One with the dry and yellow land.
Even the baobab only send forth leaves
Three months a year,
Aged ents too tired to green this dusty world.
A few carmine bee eaters
Briefly slash the dry air with bright color
In this barren terrain
Where giraffes and lions disappear
And elephant boulders
Shuffle slowly to a watering hole
To bathe in mud.
It's quieter, too, than I had thought—
The silence thick and lazy,
A lion sleeping under a stagnant blue sky.

Caminito–La Boca[1]

She stumbles along,
Dowdy in lace
And dusty with age
Abruptly pausing in a slow
Tango duplet rhythm
Remembered from her youth.
Her reticulated face,
Streaked with paint too garish,
Recalls another age,
But now her rheumy eyes don't see
The rusty ships or hear the shredded rhythms of their life.
Wrapped in guitar riffs,
Stale smoke,
Cheap perfume,
And coda dreams,
She, unstayed and bent,
Lurches to a worn and threadbare rest.

1. La Boca ("the mouth") is an old Italian neighborhood in Buenos
Aires at the mouth of the Matanza River. The buildings are painted
in a variety of bright colors. The story is that the men who worked
painting the ships would use any paint remaining after the job to
paint the houses. Rarely are the colors consistent for the entire
house Today the houses are looking a bit shabby.

Zimbabwe

Unscarred by dry and dusty poverty,
She sings and laughs,
Washing warm clothes on her front steps
In a bright plastic basin,
A daily labor.
Glory-touched, she sings hymns of praise,
And wrings each blouse or pants
Then, lifting clean wet hands,
She drapes each precious piece
On lines carefully drawn between poles—
Suspended to face the relentless sun,
Tongues of fire in a world baptized in dust.
Looking up, she sees me sitting quietly in the car
Watching her at her labors.
Joy covers her like a dress, clean and wondrous,
As she smiles and waves,
Touching my life with her grace.

Time

Chronos moves lockstep,
Certain.
It can be told by pendulum swing—
Sure footed.
One can trust its certitude.
Tethered to a watch.

Kairos, unaware of pattern,
Moves to no set rules,
Hears no rhythmic beat.
It recognizes that five minutes
Of searing pain
Has no commonality with
Five minutes with a friend.
In one, time slows to a molasses reality.
The other passes before a breath.
When reading, writing, or painting,
I surface
Only to discover
Lunch missed
And dinner running late.

Time floats by different laws—
Racing as in a monsoon
Or undulating gently
As a raft floating in a lazy sun.

Words

English, a peripatetic language,[1]
Collects words the way others bring trinkets
Home from vacations.
Consider her background—
Two complete languages
(Anglo-Saxon and Norman French).
She willingly scavenges and even
Dumpster dives in her peregrination
Search for words.
Over the years she's brought home
And adopted
Coffee, sherbet, assassin, kamikaze, giraffe
 And, given the journeys, odyssey.
She even resurrected Latin
(adding Greek here and there)
To use in medicine and science.
Latin makes it weightier,
More intelligent sounding.
Still ravenous, she even stoops to creating words
Jargon, Kleenex, laser, radar.
No rules of spelling and pronunciation hold.
But a writer has a glorious palette
With which to write a poem.

1. 2020 estimates indicate English has 1,057,380 words. The next
largest language (German) is estimated at 500,000.

Lumbricus Terrestris

For Marty

"Today we dissect Lumbricus terrestris,
The earthworm," she said,
    ᵈ the smell of formaldehyde
    ᴸted the words like lead.
Eac lace was carefully set—
A tray, napkins, utensils.
Why is biology always before lunch?
"...one long cut down the middle
Then tack the skin back so you can see inside."
It lay there pink and corrugated in horizontal segments
Like corduroy...
Except for that, it could have been a clay rope
From first grade art.
Which end was head?
Which side was up?
Give me an angle to bisect instead;
It has more certitude
And never disturbs my lunch.

Nunc Dimittis

The promise pierced my youth
Shouting glory and hope.
I'm joint twisted now,
And in my Temple wait
Messiah hopes grow dim.
Silence has become my winter cloak.
Waiting is hard.
I'm growing deaf in silence and in age.
Suddenly a Child, a Wonder,
The Light of God,
And I whisper,
"Lord, now let this servant depart
For these eyes of mine have seen
The Savior".

With deep appreciation to Sharon P. Granston, a faithful
witness who led me to right theology.

With heartfelt gratitude to Bobbie Fetzer, the prod that
convinced me to gather these poems into a book.

And thank you Gregg and Karen Rummel for the cover
design, text layout, and managing to wrestle it all to print.

Cover photo by Elizabeth L. Hudgins

CPSIA information can be obtained
at www.ICGtesting.com
Printed in the USA
BVHW012359281121
622518BV00002BA/64